LU HUNG NIEN: THE LANTERN FESTIVAL

A lantern festival heralds the Chinese New Year and takes on an added beauty in this picture through the dedication of the festival to Christian ideals in today's renaissance of Christian art.

Each with His Own Brush

Contemporary Christian Art
in Asia and Africa

by DANIEL JOHNSON FLEMING

Professor Emeritus, Union Theological Seminary, New York

Friendship Press • New York

BOOKS BY DANIEL JOHNSON FLEMING

CHRISTIAN SYMBOLS IN A WORLD COMMUNITY

*with two hundred and twenty illustrations of the way in
which non-European art forms are being adapted to the
uses of Christian symbolism*

THE WORLD AT ONE IN PRAYER

*being a collection of modern prayers by Christians in
Asia and Africa and the isles of the sea, revealing a one-
ness beneath cultural differences*

BUILDING WITH INDIA
WHAT WOULD YOU DO?
HELPING PEOPLE GROW
VENTURES IN SIMPLER LIVING
WHITHER BOUND IN MISSIONS
BRINGING OUR WORLD TOGETHER
SOCIAL STUDY, SERVICE AND EXHIBITS
WAYS OF SHARING WITH OTHER FAITHS
CONTACTS WITH NON-CHRISTIAN CULTURES
ETHICAL ISSUES CONFRONTING WORLD CHRISTIANS
DEVOLUTION IN MISSION ADMINISTRATION
SCHOOLS WITH A MESSAGE IN INDIA
ATTITUDES TOWARD OTHER FAITHS
MARKS OF A WORLD CHRISTIAN
LIVING AS COMRADES
HERITAGE OF BEAUTY

*First Printing October 1938
Second Printing April 1939
Third Printing October 1939
Fourth Printing May 1941
Fifth Printing January 1946
Sixth Printing October 1952*

ACKNOWLEDGMENTS

FOR EXTENSIVE and invaluable help in making it possible to present these pictures the author is especially indebted to Mrs. Theodore Greene, American Mission, Peking; Mrs. J. Martin Benade, American Presbyterian Mission, Lahore; and the Reverend C. P. Garman, Christian Literature Society, Tokyo. He is greatly indebted, also, to Mr. Maurice Lavanaux, secretary of the Liturgical Arts Society, New York; President W. B. Pettus, College of Chinese Studies, Peking; Miss Louise Strong Hammond, formerly of St. Luke's Studio, Nanking; and Mrs. Thomas Hobbs, Seoul, Korea. The author gratefully acknowledges help from scores of others who gave clues to pictures, sent notes on artists, or gave descriptions of their works.

The various pictures are reproduced through the courtesy and generous cooperation of the following:

China: 16, the Reverend Archibald G. Adams; 17-19, St. Luke's Studio, Nanking; 20, 21, the Reverend C. W. McDouall, Church of England Mission, Peking, owner; 22-39, The Catholic University, Peking.

Japan: 42-44, Fr. Hermann Heuvers, Sophia University, Tokyo; 45, 51, Agenzia Fides, Rome; 46, 48-50, Liturgical Arts, New York; 47, Miss Charlotte De Forest, Tokyo; 52, Toyohiko Kagawa and Mr. Kiyoshi; 53, Mr. Kiyoshi and the Reverend C. P. Garman.

India: 56, Y.M.C.A. Publishing House, Calcutta, owned by the Rt. Hon. Lord Vestey; 55, 59, 60, 63, 64, the artist, Alfred D. Thomas; 57, Father W. Q. Lash, C.P.S.S. Ashram, Poona; 58, the Reverend M. P. Davis, owner, and the Committee on Christian Literature for Women and Children in Mission Fields, Inc.; 61, Mr. J. V. Ubale; 62, Sir Henry Gidney, I.M.S., Calcutta, owner; 65, Dr. and Mrs. L. H. Beals, Wai, Western India; 66, United Missionary Girls' High School, Calcutta.

Africa: 70, 76, photograph by E. H. Duckworth, courtesy of Principal W. N. Tolfree; 71, 72, the Reverend H. P. Thompson, S.P.G., London, and Sister Pauline, C.R.; 73, The Baptist Missionary Society, London; 74, Agenzia Fides, Rome; 75, The Museum of the University of Pennsylvania; 77, *Le Bulletin des Missions,* Abbaye de S. André-lez, Bruges (Belgium).

Miscellaneous: 79, Mr. A. Chester Beatty, London, owner; 80, Agenzia Fides, Rome; 81, Mrs. Thomas Hobbs; 82, the Reverend Paul A. Eakin; 83, Mr. Gonzalo Báez Camargo and the Reverend J. P. Hauser; 84, Dr. S. C. van Randwijck, Batavia.

CONTENTS

CONTENTS

CONTENTS

INTRODUCTION

INDIGENOUS CHRISTIAN PAINTING

SOMETIMES a new and thrilling country is opened up for us to explore. It is hoped that the reproductions of indigenous Christian paintings contained in this book may afford such an adventure. It seems that we can go nowhere on this planet without finding traces of man's creative spirit, for artistic taste has been so inborn in him that, even in remote caves or when hard pressed in catacombs, this spirit has found expression. Art has always been the handmaid of religion and, in turn, religion has been the creator and preserver of art, as has been especially true in Europe. Now that Christianity has become ecumenical (or, in the literal sense of this word, has gained a foothold in all parts of the inhabited earth), one expectantly surveys the younger Christian communities of the world to see what use the church has made of form and color in the expression of her life and faith. This expansion of Christianity into the non-Christian world opens up a new significant period, not only in the expression of the spirit but also in art.

Just as we are surprised by fresh new insights gained from reading the Bible in some modern translation—in French or German, or in Hindustani or Chinese—so a sympathetic survey of these interpretations of the Christian faith in varied cultures may enrich our own appreciation. Moreover, such a survey may keep us from being parochial, may help us to understand Christian art in a truly catholic spirit since we become acquainted, not only with various characteristic stylistic differentiations, sequences and techniques, but also with new values and insights among the art treasures which each race brings for the enrichment of the church. Even a quick turning of these pages will reveal reflections of varied cultures showing that the church is stranger to no soil or country.

As at Pentecost, Parthians, Medes and Elamites heard the message, "every man in his own tongue wherein he was born," so we see Chinese and Japanese and Indian expressing Christianity's universal language, each with his own brush. For when the spirit of God descends upon any people, new forms of beauty appear, new artistic gifts are revealed, adding another testimony to the universality of the Christian faith. In particular, one is impressed by the ecumenical appeal of the theme of the nativity, for, just as it has been a favorite

1

subject for Western art down through the centuries, contemporaneous Christian artists the world around seem to delight to reveal the innocence, love and spirit of service embodied in the Virgin Mother.

Just before Epiphany, or Good Friday, or in connection with some parable, we might turn to relevant pictures and let them make our thought of the Christ more universal. Or, imagining we are in the position of consultants in any given country, we may attempt to decide which pictures, if any, we would discourage as missing a true Christian interpretation; which we would justify as being distinctly edifying or didactic, possibly as a Biblia Pauperum for the unlearned such as Christian artists began to paint in the fifth and sixth centuries; and which we would approve mainly because of the sheer artistic satisfaction they give. In order to grasp the ultimate burden of a given picture, rather than merely to like or to dislike it, we shall doubtless wish to learn whether these artists of various lands are thinking the same thoughts, merely expressing them in their own ways; or whether they represent diverse interpretations of the Christian faith. In our aspiration to develop an ecumenical Christian consciousness, we may not be able to visit in person the various areas of our world Christian community; but we can through art expand our imaginations and increase the flexibility of our minds, so that we can pass without a jar and with genuine appreciation from one regional artistic expression to another.

One of the obvious gains for the younger churches from indigenous Christian art is that it helps to remove the foreign aspect of Christianity. It helps to dissipate the deadly prejudice which regards the church as an alien cult. In these days of excessive nationalism the more our universal faith can be freed from its distinctively Western accessories the less likely is it to be boycotted in some anti-Western trend. That there are Western accessories is manifest when an African priest can say that "for the Bantu to be a Christian was to behave like a white man," or when we are told that a Madonna of the Italian type, holding her baby in a way unknown to an African mother, remains an alien.

One way of bringing about this naturalization of Christianity so much needed and well justified is to use, in the various arts, forms and techniques which are native to any given people—to use their artistic language just as already we use their literary language. For example, the Reverend H. P. Thompson tells how, at Kronstad, a black Babe was placed in the Christmas crib, thus making it quite natural for the African boys and girls to think of the Holy

Child as one of them. It was in no less concrete terms, though doubtless with a figurative meaning, that an Oxford-educated Indian put the matter: "You have brought us a Christ wearing a hat and trousers; we want to see him in a turban and *dhoti*." The pictures in this book show that a very real beginning has been made in giving national color to the Gospels; these paintings may encourage others who have the artist's gifts to use the brush they know best in portraying the life and teachings of our Lord.

But while there is a definite gain in having pictures with a genuine indigenous flavor, merely introducing an Indian or an African into a biblical scene with local background does not make a *religious* picture. Ideally such a picture would make visible Absolute Beauty in the common ways of life. Ever since the Word became flesh, this has come within the scope of artistic effort in a way unparalleled before. Such a picture would emphasize not scene but meaning— and the essential meaning of Christianity is the witness to the world of the divine and human realities as revealed in Jesus Christ. Accommodation to a particular culture is secondary to the imparting of a specifically Christian meaning—and this presupposes that the artist has caught the meaning. Important as it is to express Christianity in Japanese or Indian modes, the first essential is to know and experience what it is saying to mankind.

This puts a great responsibility upon one who aspires to be creative in the sphere of Christian art. He must not only be above the average in powers of observation, assembling and composing; he should also have deeper Christian insight, feeling and experience. The extent to which this is true for the artists whose works are here shown may be judged, for in their original form these productions would give (as has been said of all pictures) "indubitable witness to the moral state of the painter at the moment when he takes his brush." Any artist, East or West, who essays Christian themes might learn from Wang Li, a Chinese artist of the fourteenth century, who painted the Hua mountain in Shensi. Dr. A. K. Coomaraswamy, in the *New Orient,* quotes Wang Li: "Until I knew the shape of the Hua mountain how could I paint a picture of it? But even after I had visited it and drawn it from nature, the 'idea' was still immature. Subsequently I brooded upon it in the quiet of my house, on my walks abroad, in bed and at meals, at concerts, in intervals of conversation and of literary composition. One day when I was resting I heard drums and flutes passing the door. I leapt up and cried, 'I have it.' Then I tore up my old sketches, and painted it again. This time my only guide was the Hua mountain, itself."

3

INDIGENOUS CHRISTIAN PAINTING

There is a high demand, also, on all those who undertake to look at pictures coming out of another culture. It is hardly enough to admire only what at first sight appeals to our taste, or reasonable to quarrel with an artist because of some omission which his national esthetic does not demand. For example, it never occurs to a primitive African that imitative likeness to nature is either possible or desirable—his attention is on something else. For any fair appraisal some preparation, therefore, may be necessary—a discovery that one's own cultural patterns are themselves relative, and that no people's modes of expression are curiously quaint to that people. Therefore, if these pictures seem exotic to us, it may mean that we have not yet entered into any real community of feeling with our "neighbors." To the extent permitted by the limited space beneath each picture an attempt has been made to help in this appreciation. But the author must leave any extended criticism to those more artistically qualified.

Indigenous art, however, is still in its infancy. The Reverend John J. Considine, assistant general of the Catholic Foreign Mission Society of America, summarizing the whole movement toward indigenous art in the Roman Catholic church, writes in *Liturgical Arts*: "Compared with the vast proportions of the mission world, the amount of existing local Christian art is relatively small, and except in a few cases, as yet it is not outstanding from the viewpoint of quality. It is the idea which is great. It is the dream of tomorrow, rather than the spectacle of today, which makes enthusiasm."

This judgment from an outstanding Roman Catholic authority was confirmed by many an answer to the scores of letters sent out in connection with this study. Amongst the younger churches, Christian art is undoubtedly furthest advanced in China; and yet Dr. Y. Y. Tsu, the present chairman of the Church Art Society (page 11), which has been struggling for years to develop Chinese Christian art, can write: "Christian symbolism and themes are new in this field, and it will take time for our people to become familiar with and to develop an appreciation of them. At present, there is no widespread public for the works of Chinese painters even within the church itself, and none outside it. The works so far produced are little better than what is known among connoisseurs as 'artisan' grade, and mainly intended for pedagogic purposes in religious education. When an outstanding Chinese artist who has an independently established name turns his energy and attention to the development of Christian themes, then Chinese Christian art will receive recognition as art."

INDIGENOUS CHRISTIAN PAINTING

In the light of these statements it seems less strange to hear from the president of a theological seminary in India: "I fear that art has not been very much encouraged in our Christian work." From Korea: "There has been so little development along this line, and the few examples available are so mediocre, that no one would wish them to represent Korean artistic ability." From Siam: "So far as I know, there are no indigenous Christian pictures in this country. For pictorial presentation of the life and teachings of Jesus, dependence has been placed upon foreign models." From Mexico: "Roman Catholic pictures are of distinctly Spanish or European style. The Protestant church, at first, felt it necessary to eliminate all religious art. As yet it has produced no religious pictures in non-European style. The renaissance of Indian influence in Mexican art is confined to the so-called 'proletarian,' often anti-Christian, painters." From another Spanish area comes this word: "Filipino art is frankly and unblushingly an imitation of European art." From Hawaii: "Music, drama, simple craft work, and the colorfulness of their surroundings seem to satisfy these people. Native Hawaiians do not have any contribution, past or present, in the realm of painting." From Uganda: "No attempt has been made to use indigenous art in the service of the church. The African here has not yet felt free to tackle biblical subjects in an unconventional and real way." From the Congo: "There is absolutely nothing original in the way of religious art depicted in this area." From the secretary of a society working in Nigeria and Ethiopia: "The church has not developed to the place where there is a native art." Similar quotations, made of course without exhaustive investigation, could be given from other areas. Disillusioning as are these appraisals of indigenous Christian art, we must not let ourselves disbelieve in the certainty of its appearance. Any spiritual movement which is destined for dominance or survival will, in due time, find expression in the arts.

There are various causes of this backwardness—some avoidable, some inherent in the situation. Most art has been the product of stable and independent civilizations; societies strained by the impact of modern industrialism and by Western civilization are distinctly handicapped. Art is generally fostered by the wealthy and the learned; but the Christian communities are not wealthy and, in general, do not contain many men and women versed in the higher art and culture of their respective countries. As one thinks of relatively small Christian communities, pressed upon by pervasive non-Christian environments, one finds another reason in the fact that great periods of art have been the expression of their times. These great periods have embodied not the dreams of individuals but the hopes of a nation; they have been nourished and inspired by tides of thought and emotion. How different the whole milieu which conditions the struggling Christian minorities! We must acknowledge, also, that Christianity has been mediated by men and women who, however highly equipped with the culture of their Western lands, in many cases have not been deeply acquainted with, or, alas, even concerned about, the indigenous culture of the lands to which they go. That there should be as much creativity on the part of nationals as is indicated in this book is under the circumstances a matter of wonder.

There is one obstacle that Western Christians and churches might well help to remove. Later we will hear of a Chinese artist of rare talent who, when in dire need of money for medical attention, failed to find purchasers for his pictures. Again, the church in India has found an artist of deep insight and devotion, who desires to give all his time to Christian art, but the Christian community in India is too poor to absorb his work. We will hear of an art guild which has been struggling for ten years to get an endowment that would help its work of fostering the talents of local Christian artists. Obviously indigenous art is needed by the younger churches; but would not homes and churches in the West be enriched by some beautiful originals by an Eastern artist? Such originals are not only available, but their sale in the more wealthy West is almost a matter of life or death for Christian art in several lands.

There are manifold dangers and difficulties in the development of indigenous Christian art. If a foreigner attempts to transpose himself creatively into the cultural background of another people he may produce a Madonna dressed in colors that would be worn by a dancing girl; or he may make a chasuble (as was done by early Jesuits in Java) on which is a design ordinarily employed only on a woman's kain or skirt and hence, to the cultured Javanese mind, out of place on an article of worship; or "The Light of the World" may be drawn with the figure carrying a tea-house lantern. It takes intimate study and rare imaginative capacity to succeed when venturing to use another's esthetic language.

The surest procedure seems to be to awaken artistic creativeness among the nationals themselves. Here, also, there are surprises. In a Chinese presentation of the story of the prodigal son, the father is shown sitting on the verandah waiting to receive the son. When it was pointed out that the father "ran to meet him," it was replied that no Chinese father would do that—and so one of the deepest points was missed. On the other hand, a Japanese artist did not want to paint the return at all, "for no Japanese youth would think of coming back penniless to a father; and a father would be disgraced to have his child come back that way." The chairman of a competition in India tells of one picture which was submitted "depicting our Lord looking like a florid Englishman with red hair, bright blue eyes, highly colored cheeks, and lips as though painted with the brightest lipstick obtainable." In Japan a beautiful scroll-picture of the Crucifixion was painted to order—but the features were exactly those of a Buddha in absorption. In the first sketch of the carving, "All Creatures Praising God," on page 76, the African artist portrayed a fish in the crocodile's mouth; his adviser had to point out that the crocodile could not, and the fish would not, praise God under those circumstances! These, doubtless, are exceptional illustrations. They show not only that when indigenous art is encouraged one must be ready for unusual interpretations coming from differences in environment, historical circumstances, natural aptitude, and understanding of the crucial problems of life; they also show that, in spite of an Asiatic or African setting, the true message may be dimmed or suppressed. The artist may be more interested in adaptation than in true interpretation.

When Christianity leaves Palestine and enters another culture, a decision has to be made as to whether one should aim at historical, ethnological and archeological accuracy when painting biblical scenes, or whether local models and backgrounds may be used with the main interest liturgical or spiritual. We must remember that the West has learned to admire the works of Fra Angelico, the Van Eycks, Dürer, Rembrandt, and in our day preeminently Fritz von Uhde, without questioning the way in which they transferred the events of the New Testament to their own times. Is there not as much propriety in Chinese figures against a Chinese background? We, at least, must acknowledge inconsistency, if we concur in Italians painting Italian Madonnas, while disapproving the various characteristically Asiatic and African expressions of this theme.

Opinion is divided when it comes to portraying our Lord. All would say that whatever is historically unique in Christianity cannot submit to regional modification. But the immediate question is whether the symbolic picturing of Christ as incarnate in every land is such an unjustified modification. The problem is illustrated by the experience of a young art teacher of Foochow who painted the scene of Jesus stilling the sea. There was a majestic figure standing in the bow of a boat, with outstretched arms, and clothed in the conventional flowing robe of China's ancient style—but it was a back view. The artist explained that he wanted to paint Jesus as a Chinese but did not know how he would look, so he did not show the face. In considering what we would advise that young artist to do, let us remember that it was only eighty years ago that Millais' "Christ in the House of His Parents" was called odious, revolting and blasphemous by his contemporaries because he omitted the halo and made Jesus a boy in an English carpenter shop. This was the beginning of a nineteenth century school which, in the spirit of sincerity as well as of reverence, dared the innovation of refusing to exalt sacred scenes above the common ways of life. Various solutions to this problem will be found in the pictures of this book. Possibly some will think that the Roman Catholic church is wise in having, besides a strong ecclesiastical tradition, definite canon law ruling that no sacred picture may be printed or reproduced for public veneration or distribution without being submitted to previous ecclesiastical censorship, and that no Ordinary shall allow in church or other sacred places representations which are dogmatically incorrect, or are not executed with proper decency and respect.

This present-day dedication of old techniques and stylistic forms to the portrayal of new values and insights under the inspiration of Christianity can play a real part in helping us to see a world Christian community in the making. Let the building of the French Cathedral of Chartres be a symbol of what is taking place. It was an entire community that flowered forth in that great cathedral. All of the inhabitants, of whatever rank, brought stones for the construction of the building. The work of erection went on from generation to generation, for no one group could complete the task. Each of the various parts contributed its value to the whole. There were the pillars and arches to support; there were many sculptures embodying the story of the faith; and there was the dazzling beauty of color in those rose windows. Today, as we reflect on God in history and try to catch his overarching constructive purpose for this generation, we find him calling us to build—to build a world-wide Christian fellowship, rooted in its relationship to God through Christ, replenishing its strength through worship, filled with the spirit of service, and dependent on spiritual power even unto sacrificial self-giving. This spiritual cathedral, also, will not be completed in one generation, and to its consummation each culture must bring its distinctive gifts. May the pictures in this volume increase our expectancy that each people will have its tributes of insight and devotion to decorate the walls of the "building of God, an house not made with hands, eternal in the heavens."

This is the first attempt, so far as the author is aware, to bring together pictures of Christian paintings from various lands. He has drawn upon museums in Switzerland, Britain and America, upon private owners, upon editors, and upon certain Roman Catholic and Protestant centers promoting art by nationals. All who scan these pages will, of course, give the artists credit for far more charm in their pictures than reproductions in black and white reveal. Obviously with a limited number of reproductions possible, the selection of pictures has been typical rather than exhaustive, both in respect to artists and to countries represented. No picture painted in Europe is included because, in general, mission art has been Western art, and hence is already widely known. It is hoped that even this limited number will suggest that Christians in every land, when possessed by the Spirit of the Lord, will be impelled to use to the glory of God the artistic genius they possess.

"SPREADING THE SILK" IN CHINA

IN THE MODERN Christian compositions which follow this introduction one cannot help but catch the pleasure taken in trees, and flowers, and rocks. For nowhere in art has landscape been so central and dominant a theme as in China. Her artists never tire in portraying mountain and mist and stream, or a spray of flowering plum, or slender bamboos trembling in the wind. The mood of a Chinese artist seems to be at home with mountain solitudes and rushing torrents, and he loves to picture the small figure of a sage or a way-farer at the foot of a towering crag—possibly an unconscious symbol of his conception of the relative place of man.

Yet Christian artists are breaking with traditional Chinese painting in so far as it has become a spiritless and monotonous repetition of formal and standardized motifs. They are blending classical formulæ with a wealth of Christian themes. In this new way of "spreading the silk"—an old Chinese way of describing the painter's art—they are confident that they are helping Chinese painting to flower afresh, bringing to it an inexhaustible fund of inspiration.

Early in the Buddhist approach to China extensive religious use was made of Chinese art forms in sculpture, painting and architecture, making a profound impression on the Chinese people. But although Christianity entered China at least thirteen hundred years ago, so far as is known no great use was made of Chinese art for Christian purposes until the past fifty years. Most of it has been produced within the last two decades by both Protestants and Roman Catholics. It seems appropriate that the nation which has done so much for art should give to the world through this medium its interpretation of things Christian.

The Nestorian Christians who went to China in the seventh century ex-pressed themselves artistically, so far as we know, only in enlisting one of the best calligraphists of the T'ang dynasty to write the characters cut on the famous Nestorian Monument in Sianfu. No artistic remains have been found of the Roman Catholic missionaries who served in Peking during the thirteenth and fourteenth centuries—the second great period of Christianity in China.

During the third great period of Christianity in China (the seventeenth and eighteenth centuries) the brilliant group of Jesuits included several very able artists who learned to paint in Chinese style. The Chinese art historians themselves connect with the name of the great Jesuit, Matteo Ricci (1583), the introduction of foreign influence on indigenous art. Only a few examples of Christian painting of these centuries are known today—possibly one result of anti-Christian persecutions which closed this period.

Among the earliest modern Chinese Christian paintings are those in the hospital of the Church Missionary Society, Hangchow, produced a few years before 1900. (See pages 14, 15.)

In 1926 there was started at Nanking an art society known as St. Luke's Studio (Episcopal), with the object of encouraging creative art in the Chinese church. The inspiration for this movement came when the Reverend T. K. Shen (now Bishop Shen of Shensi), who is himself an artist of high standard, discovered that a new convert to Christianity to whom he was administering baptism, Mr. S. C. Hsü, was also an artist, as well as holding a position on the railway. Mr. Hsü had never heard of Chinese Christian art; hence his contact with Bishop Shen opened up a whole new world to him. He became a devout and faithful Christian. In his art work, in true Chinese fashion, he enlisted the help of his own old teacher, a proficient non-Christian painter, so the resulting pictures are especially interesting as giving the first impressions of the gospel story on Chinese minds trained in other art traditions. The pictures were, however, repeatedly criticized by Bishop Shen, Mrs. I. L. Hammond, an American artist, and others, before being put in final form. (See pages 17-19.)

Hand-painted copies of the St. Luke's Studio paintings have been made available, as well as Christmas cards, hand-colored by young women under the supervision of Bishop Shen's mother. The welcome they have received has been most encouraging, and many such copies may be found in different parts of China and abroad.

In 1934 the Studio became the Church Art Society, of which Bishop Shen was the first president, its purpose being to pioneer in giving spontaneous racial expression to Christian devotion for the Chinese church. The Church Art Society has so far produced mainly such church furnishings as altar crosses, candlesticks and hangings, and books covered with the famous Nanking tapestry, woven especially for the Society with Christian designs.

Up to the present time, by far the most extensive and successful effort to develop Chinese Christian art was made under the enthusiastic stimulus of His Excellency, Archbishop Costantini, first apostolic delegate to China (1922-

11

1933), a great lover of art. He was disappointed in finding no Roman Catholic artists or paintings and called the attention of his missionaries, therefore, to the wise rules concerning art issued by the Sacred Congregation for the Propagation of the Faith. Holding that it had always been the practice of the Roman Catholic church to adapt herself to the customs and the forms of the countries to which she had carried the faith, he urged them to have such a living sense of the catholicity of the Christian religion as would enable them to use the innumerable and delicate forms of decorative art in China's patrimony.

In 1928, while visiting an exhibition in Peking, His Excellency discovered a non-Christian artist, Ch'en Hsü, in whose work was a light of inspiration and a delicate sense for representing not so much the material object, as its poetic aspect according to the finest traditions of Chinese painting. Archbishop Costantini gave him the New Testament to read and begged him to paint his impressions, leaving him free to depict them in whatever way he pleased. Some of the best works of Western Christian art were shown him. Mr. Ch'en's study of the Gospels to be illustrated led, after several years, to his conversion (1932), the Archbishop giving him at baptism the Christian name of Luke. Mr. Ch'en writes: "I believe that when I paint the wonders of Christianity according to the ancient rules of Chinese art, the painted object exerts an externally new and strange effect, so that at the same time I enrich to a marked degree the old laws of Chinese painting. . . . If I can represent the teachings of our holy church in pictures according to Chinese art, and by means of such natural impressions draw the Chinese to know God, why should I not render so useful and enjoyable a service?" (See pages 22-26.)

Luke Ch'en became one of the professors in the Catholic University of Peking. Several of his students began the study of the Bible and the catechism and tried to fix on canvas what they had read and heard. It is significant that almost all of the original members of this school became Christians through their work in art.

Hsü Chi Hua, who recently died at the early age of twenty-five, was the second artist-convert (1932). He was known for his fervor of faith, his forbearance, and his deep religious disposition. After completing a three-year course in art he attempted to support his mother by his painting. While his pictures found many admirers, there were few purchasers. His lungs became seriously affected; his furniture traveled to the pawnshop; his Christian pictures were brought to the University officials to secure money for doctor's bills.

However, try as they might, there was no demand. During this last illness he was continually planning whole series of new religious pictures which he longed to execute after his recovery. In him, Chinese Christian art lost a promising exponent. (See pages 27, 28.)

Mr. Wang Su-Ta, the third artist-convert, comes from a strongly Buddhist family. In his ancestral home there was a well kept altar and regular sacrifices have been a fervent part of the family ritual. The Wangs for every generation have produced a painter, so that it was not surprising that this son manifested artistic talent from early childhood. While studying art a strong attraction to Christianity developed and, though vigorously denounced by his fellow painters for his thirty Christian themes, he was received into the Roman Catholic church in 1937. (See pages 36-39.)

The fourth prominent artist of this school is Lu Hung Nien, a young man of twenty-four, who is considering becoming a Christian. (See pages 30-34.)

Aggressive steps for the encouragement of Christian art are more in evidence in China than elsewhere in Asia and Africa. One hundred and eighty pictures of Christian themes have been painted by members of the Department of Fine Arts of the Catholic University. Since 1935, this university has held three exhibitions in Peking, and in 1938 assisted in exhibitions at the Eucharist Congress at Budapest, at Vienna, and in the Vatican at Rome. Bishop Shen, of St. Luke's Studio, has arranged several exhibits in Nanking, and in 1930 gave an illustrated lecture at the International Exhibit of Ecclesiastical Art in London, showing how the Christian spirit had been clothed in Chinese dress. Mrs. Theodore Greene, American Mission, Peking, has been responsible for three exhibitions of Christian paintings in recent years. Hence China's contribution to the exhibit of Christian art by the International Missionary Council, at Madras, 1938, ought to be a stimulus to many other lands.

TAI CHIEN: RETURN OF THE PRODIGAL

Luke 15:11-32

Over forty years ago two artists, father and son named Tai, painted
ten pictures of the parables. The originals (2′ x 3′) hang in the hospital of the Church Mission Society, Hangchow. In these early modern
Christian paintings there was no hesitation in introducing Chinese
figures and Chinese costumes in portraying the parables. But these
artists did not venture to represent our Lord as a Chinese.

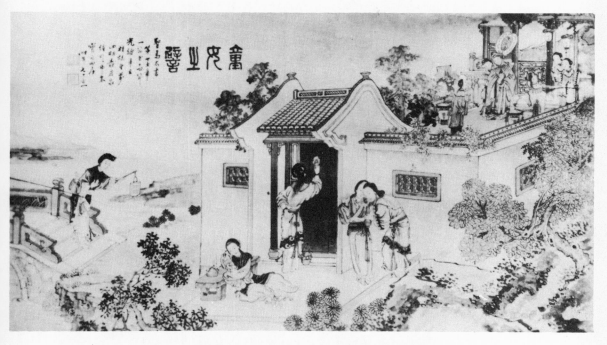

TAI EN CH'UAN: THE WISE AND FOOLISH VIRGINS

Matthew 25: 1-13

In this picture (another of the Hangchow series) is shown a Chinese courtyard with a wedding feast in progress. The five late virgins are unable to gain admission. Most of this group of pictures are too crowded to be effective to Western eyes in reproduction, but the technical skill and masterly handling of the subjects have been much admired by Chinese critics.

15

EMBARKING ON THE CHRISTIAN BOAT

Nineteen hundred miles up the Yangtze River is a little chapel at Hwen Giang, West China. On its walls was a mural painting about seven feet long. It represented Jesus and his disciples afloat on a raft which seemed to be a dragon's outspread skin. It bore an inscription: "All men who are able to embark upon this boat will enjoy happiness, and by persistently seeking the true way will happily reach heaven. Written by Chwen Lien Po in the year of Tin Chih." So far as is known no foreigner had even seen, much less influenced, the painting of this mural in far interior China until it was photographed by the Reverend Archibald G. Adams in 1916. Possibly the halo showed Buddhist influence. The mural was obliterated soon after 1916, having been on the wall probably four years.

16

聖母神子

HSU SAN CH'UN: MADONNA OF THE RISING SUN

This and the next three pictures are from St. Luke's Studio (see page 11). "The sun of righteousness" (*Malachi* 4:2) is rising over the horizon to illumine the world, betokening the coming of the Savior. It speaks of the new life and hope that came to the Orient through Christianity. Since Chinese artists were familiar with the presentation of Kwanyin, the goddess of mercy, it was relatively easy to picture Mary. But it was hard to get a satisfactory face for the Holy Child, because Chinese representations of children are rather unnatural, making them appear as little men. Many attempts were made before this picture was approved.

HSU SAN CH'UN: VISIT OF THE MAGI

Matthew 2:1-2

Under the thatch beside the pine tree are the three Magi, here symbolizing the three traditional religions of China. The kneeling figure is a Buddhist monk, as his shaven crown indicates. To the extreme right is a Confucianist, formal and correct in his dignified demeanor. Laotze, with a long beard and with a bottle of the water of mercy in his hand, represents Taoism. Joseph is on the left. Each brings his gift to the infant Jesus. This was meant to symbolize that the old revelations are not wholly discarded.

HSU SAN CH'UN: *left,* JESUS AND THE WOMAN OF SAMARIA (*John* 4:1-30);

right, WASHING THE DISCIPLES' FEET (*John* 13:1-17)

It is a Chinese custom to have four scrolls of writing on one side-wall of a guest hall, and four pictures on the opposite wall. One series chosen by Bishop Shen represented prayer, healing, preaching, and service. Two of this series are reproduced on this page— preaching and service. We see on the left a Chinese well, a Chinese bucket, and the inevitable, conventionalized rock so much appreciated in Chinese art. On the right, the artist has depicted various emotions as the Chinese disciples behold what their Master is doing. The originals are about six feet long, painted in water colors of soft and harmonious hues.

SILAS YU: PARABLE OF THE LOST COIN

Luke 15:8-10

The artist while still a schoolboy showed artistic ability, and was encouraged by the American Church Mission, Hankow. Mr. Yü eventually devoted his talent to furthering indigenous Christianity in China by painting biblical subjects. In this picture, architecture, furniture, costume and hair-dressing are all "period"—i.e., of the time of Jesus.

20

SILAS YU: DIVES AND LAZARUS

Luke 16:19-31

Note the gaudy parrot embodying the spirit of Dives. The drawn-back curtain reveals
emptiness beyond. Lazarus is seated on a stone bench and beside him is a battered tree.
But beyond is a strong new-life tree symbolic of his future. This and the preceding
picture manifestly get their effect without Western decorativeness and without Western
conventional symbolism.

21

LUKE CH'EN: STAR OF THE SEA

In Western art, as here, the Madonna is often crowned as Queen of Heaven. It will be remembered that in Murillo's "Immaculate Conception" Mary is standing upon the clouds, the crescent moon beneath her feet. This picture is sometimes called "The Madonna of the Clouds" or "The Madonna of the Crescent Moon."

The waters, the primary metaphysical symbol for potentiality or universal supply, form an interesting feature below. Moreover, a traditional motive is that of the moon over raging waves. Unlike a Western artist, who would seek to catch the actual aspect of the sea, the Chinese artist uses a convention of sinuous lines in order to communicate what he considers the essential movement—the continuity and rhythm of the waves.

22

竹宋人寺龍敗白描法
一九三七年六月 陳緣加敬繪

LUKE CH'EN: MADONNA OF THE MOON WINDOW

The moon gate and round window are always intriguing elements in
Chinese architecture, as well as in paintings. The Chinese regard the
paintings of bamboo as most near Chinese calligraphy, which is held in
even higher regard than Chinese landscape.

23

天神之后
路加陳緣督敬寫

LUKE CH'EN: QUEEN OF THE HEAVENLY CHOIR

24

LUKE CH'EN: ST. PAUL BEFORE THE ALTAR TO THE UNKNOWN GOD

Acts 17:23

25

LUKE CH'EN: GETHSEMANE

Mark 14:32-42

The Savior at prayer, his sleeping disciples, and the angel who offers the cup are all painted as Chinese. The costume is of the Confucian period — an effort to remove the scene from space and time.

HSU CHI HUA: TEACHING BY THE SEASIDE

Mark 4:1-34

27

HSU CHI HUA: THE RESURRECTION

Luke 24

YUEH HAN CHAN PENG: MADONNA OF THE
SNOWY WILLOW TREE

29

LU HUNG NIEN: NO ROOM IN THE INN

Luke 2:7

Mary stands in the snow in the foreground, while Joseph knocks
at the gate. He carries their scanty effects in a bundle, Chinese
fashion, on the end of a stick. The barking dog, the boy waving
his hands, and the innkeeper not even leaving his table show the
lack of preparation for the visitors.

30

LU HUNG NIEN: THE HOLY FAMILY IN WINTER

Chinese artists love to depict the different seasons. Hence, not a few Christian themes are found in a series of spring, summer, autumn, winter. This picture is from such a series. Joseph is coming home. On his back is a typical carpenter's kit in which one can see an ax and saw—the tools most commonly used.

LU HUNG NIEN: FLIGHT INTO EGYPT

Matthew 2:13-14

The flight is represented as taking place in a small boat, poled by a
fisherman. Joseph is seated in the stern.

32

LU HUNG NIEN: THE GOOD SAMARITAN

Luke 10:30-37

The rescue takes place in a mountain gorge. The priest and
Levite can be seen in the distance.

33

LU HUNG NIEN: JESUS AND THE WOMAN OF SAMARIA

John 4:1-30

The well is under a Chinese thatch with a walled city and mountains
covered with snow as background.

34

CH'EN LU CHIA: DIVES AND LAZARUS

Luke 16:19-31

The bamboo is strong and tough, yet yielding. When bowed down
with the weight of snow it springs back to its former position. This
suggestion of the way adversity should be borne is the background for
this parable. There are detailed and elaborate treatises in China solely
devoted to the subject of bamboo painting. An artist will concentrate
on this subject for many years until the leaves seem wet with dew
and trembling in the wind.

WANG SU-TA· MADONNA AND CHILD

36

WANG SU-TA: JESUS WITH MARTHA AND MARY

Luke 10:38-42

37

WANG SU-TA: JESUS CALMING THE STORM
Mark 4:35-39

38

WANG SU-TA: CALVARY

Luke 23:33-46

OLD TECHNIQUES FOR NEW THEMES
IN JAPAN

In Japan, before the advent of Buddhism in the sixth century, Shinto worship was very simple and was conducted without the use of images. Buddhism brought an immense addition to religious thought and a wealth of art in architecture and ritual with which to express its worship. This art had its origin in India, and was enriched by its passage through China and Korea on its way to Japan. Professor Anesaki, of the Imperial University, Tokyo, writes: "For the first time they saw the figure of a divine being reproduced in beauty, and adored by means of elaborate rituals. This was indeed a new revelation which was destined to rule the faith and sentiment of the nation. . . . Buddhist art was the most effective means of attracting the people's admiration and reverence to religion."

Developed through the centuries, art in its many forms is now one of the glories of Japan. It excels in pictures of nature and the forces of nature, portrayed with extraordinary vividness and power. Animals and flowers are interpreted with tenderness and sensibility. Until recent times the human form and the human face were not the center of interest. Where figures appear now, it is their activity which arrests attention rather than their person.

There are various reasons why Christian painting has been backward in Japan. Poverty and relatively small numbers have limited the church. Japanese preference for pictures of nature has been mentioned. Like the Chinese they enjoy art in their written characters—a formal, esthetic expression most Westerners have not learned to appreciate—so that a well chosen and well written saying gives as much pleasure as a picture. Furthermore, until recently, Japanese Christians have made a complete break, not only with Buddhism but with the architecture and the artistic expressions associated with Buddhism. As Christians, they are at home with Western forms. In time, however, just as Buddhism coming in from without helped art to flower forth in Japan, so Christianity will doubtless bring a new joy and freshness of soul, rejuvenating techniques many centuries old, permitting one to see what this art of the Far East can be under the breath of the Holy Spirit. Where the Spirit of the Lord is, there is liberty.

A slight change is taking place, though Japanese Christian art is still in its infancy and not yet generally popular. Some ten years ago a little group of Japanese artists founded the Catholic Artists' Guild and have done some interesting work, particularly in the field of painting. They have held several expositions in Tokyo. Even in the pictures by artists of this guild (pages 42, 43, 45, 46, 49-51), however, Western influence is strongly evident. Examples from the growing number of Protestant artists, also, are given (pages 44, 47, 52, 53). In all the great exhibitions of art, such as the one at Ueno (Tokyo), each autumn one will find one or more striking pictures of Christian themes attracting much attention.

So far as the data revealed by this study show, Japanese Christian artists have done more than those in any other non-Western land to enrich the church of today by recalling the most ennobling events in their own early Christian history. The beginnings of Christianity in any land have incidents of heroism, sacrifice or devotion which should be made to live on in art, not only for the land concerned, but also for the church universal.

Possibly few realize that Japan was the scene of one of the most remarkable adventures that Christianity has had—the Roman Catholic entrance and work in Japan, 1549-1638. The zealous Francis Xavier with his fellow Jesuits began the work, followed by members of other orders. Numerous converts were gained, so that Christianity became in an amazing way a factor to be taken into account by government and people. But the missionaries became involved in political intrigues. Well justified fear spread that Christians would be used as the opening wedge for conquest by Spaniards or Portuguese. Exceedingly severe persecution began. Christians were subjected to tortures, but were released if they would step upon a "Tramping Board" upon which was a crucifix. In 1638, after practically eradicating Christianity from the country, Japan definitely cut itself off from European intercourse, and not until two and a half centuries had passed were the edict boards prohibiting Christianity removed in Japan. (See pages 48-51.)

TAKAHIRA TODA: THE VISITATION OF MARY

Luke 1:39

The artist comes from a family of Buddhist priests and painters. It is not strange, therefore, that he developed a special devotion to Kwannon (the Japanese goddess of mercy). It was just this similarity between Kwannon and the Virgin that led to Mr. Toda's interest in Christianity, and eventually to his becoming a catechumen of the Roman Catholic church.

In this picture, painted on silk, Mary is on her way "into the hill country" to visit Elizabeth. In the reproduction one misses the delicate colors of the hills, the red bodice, and the slender golden outlinings of the embroidery in the original.

KIMI KOSEKI: BABYHOOD OF OUR LORD

Miss Koseki comes from Sendai. Her father was an army officer and she was
left an orphan while still quite young. She was able, however, to study at the
Imperial Art School, and entered the Roman Catholic church while there. She
has won a reputation for the portrayal of the countryside of northern Japan.
This picture represents the motherly care in Bethlehem as it would have occurred
near Sendai. Though still a young woman, Miss Koseki has had pictures in five
Autumn Academy exhibitions.

43

YOKEI SADAKATA: "COME UNTO ME"

In this picture there is the suggestion of a Japanese face, and the robe is closely related to that of a Buddhist priest; yet there is a manifest attempt by the artist to produce something universal. In the palm of each hand appear lines delineating a cross. Mr. Sadakata is an outstanding artist and a devout Methodist. He feels that painting in the Christian tradition is a form of worship, and that when he paints on Sunday he is receiving the support of the worshipping Christians of the world.

44

YOKEI SADAKATA: THE FIRST TEMPTATION

A large problem in the naturalization of Christianity—far larger than expression in art—
is illustrated by this picture. Opinion will doubtless be divided. Some will highly
approve, not alone because of the artistic merits of the picture, but because it is a
representation of Jesus in the dress, posture and spirit of the highest a convert has known
in Buddhism. Others may say that this is a precise illustration of the dangers of syncre-
tism. Jesus did not separate himself from the world in passive meditation; he did not
attempt to eliminate all desire as did Buddha; he came not to be ministered unto, but to
minister. Such critics would say that this picture is definitely in the axis of Buddhism,
not in the axis of Christianity, and therefore is a type of picture not to be encouraged
in the indigenous church.

45

LUKE HASEGAWA: GETHSEMANE

Matthew 26:36-46

The artist was a pupil in a school of the Marianist Brothers, where he became a Christian.
After studying in the Imperial Art School, Tokyo, he was sent by the government to
Europe to study the art of fresco painting.

SABURO TAKASHIMA: THE CRUCIFIXION

Luke 23:33-46

Saburo Takashima was a son of the well known artist, Hokkai Takashima, and studied engineering. But before graduating from the university he came down with tuberculosis and after eight years of invalidism died in 1932. His mother was an earnest Christian. During his illness his faith greatly developed, and also he discovered that he had some of his father's artistic gift. As he developed this gift, he set out to make a complete set of pictures of the life of Christ. He executed only five, however, and of these the last was "The Crucifixion."

47

MADAME TAKAHASHI: PERSECUTION OF CHRISTIANS

Madame Takahashi gives dramatic expression to the ever varying theme of martyrdom, known to every Japanese Christian today. In the foreground mothers with their daughters are called upon to renounce their faith by stepping on the "Tramping Board" to the left (see page 41). In the background appear the boats destined to carry away their husbands and brothers into exile.

SEIKYO OKAYAMA: FIVE JAPANESE MARTYRS

Seikyo Okayama comes from a family with a tradition as priests of Shinto
shrines. He became interested in the history of Christian martyrs in Japan.
While teaching at a school in Kyushu he studied the local Christian relics.
This led to an interest in Christianity and to his conversion as a Roman
Catholic. He has sent many pictures representing Japanese martyrs to the
Lateran Museum in Rome. From left to right the martyrs are Leonia,
Martha who became blind in prison, Paul Miki, Ludovico Ibaraki, and
Magdalen of the third order of St. Dominic.

SUJAKU SUZUKI: GRATIA HOSOKAWA

The wife of a prominent seventeenth century *daimyo,* named Hosokawa, eluded mansion guards to visit a church. Christian instruction was often sent to her from a Jesuit priest through a trusty maid. Ere long she and sixteen of her maids were baptized. Her tragic end came in 1600 during civil war. Below and around the border one can see enemies of the *daimyo* storming the castle. She is kneeling before a crucifix and in the presence of her steward, who has been instructed to take her life lest she be captured as a hostage by the enemy.

LUKE HASEGAWA: A JAPANESE MARTYR

A *samurai,* or military retainer, is kneeling over his victim, whose heroic death has been the means of bringing him the Faith. The artist has had exhibits in the Lateran Museum, Rome.

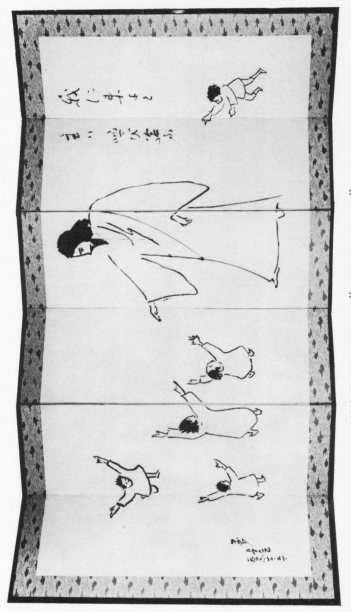

TOYOHIKO KAGAWA: "COME UNTO ME"

Matthew 19:13-15

Friends of Kagawa the world over think of him as a prophet of social justice, as a great organizer of co-operatives, as a prolific author, or as "the greatest gift of Japan to the universal church." This six-leaf screen, showing children answering the call of Jesus, gives a glimpse of how this great lover of men expresses his Christian longing and evangelistic zeal with a painter's brush.

52

TEIJI HIRAZAWA: GRACE BEFORE MEALS

Two figures, seated in Japanese fashion before the low Japanese table, are asking God's blessing on their evening meal. The artist is a well known Protestant who draws illustrations for some of Dr. Toyohiko Kagawa's publications as well as for other Christian literature issued in Japan.

PAINTING THE "HYMN OF THE LORD"
IN INDIA

INDIAN ART has been predominantly religious. The saying, "You cannot sing anything but the hymn of the Lord," might be applied to the whole range of India's esthetic expression. But a truly Indian interpretation of Christian themes through the medium of Indian art has been long delayed, though recognized as one of the needs of the Indian church. It is not altogether strange that Christian painting has not come to birth sooner, for in India the art of making pictures at all has only in recent years been revived, after long disuse. Now a truly national school of art is evolving, as distinctive as that of China or of Japan.

There has arisen in North India a young Indian Christian who has a definite vocation to art, Mr. Alfred David Thomas. In his work, more than in that of any other one painter, the Christian church of India has at last found artistic expression. The Christian training of his childhood has been his inspiration in later life, and his subjects are largely those of the Bible. Mr. Thomas has studied art in Lucknow, Calcutta, and Florence, and hence his style is a combination of Indian and Italian. Though only thirty years of age, Mr. Thomas is soon to make his third trip to art centers in Europe.

An outstanding experiment in providing low-cost pictures in color for the Christian church has been made by the Committee on Christian Literature for Women and Children in Mission Fields, Inc. (New York), in co-operation with the National Christian Council of India. The Committee's secretary, Miss Clementina Butler, heard that cheap pictures of Hindu religious themes and gods were abundantly available in color, and that such pictures were sometimes found on the walls of the mud huts of village Christians. When, in explanation, they answered, "We do not believe in these stories any longer, but the pictures are pretty," she resolved to do something about it. Several outstanding Western pictures, each with a single clear-cut idea as in "The Good Shepherd," were reproduced. But there was the fear that Western symbolism might be unintelligible and that such pictures would too much associate Christianity with white supremacy. For the past four years, therefore, prizes for Christian pictures by Indian artists have been offered. The picture on page 58 is one of those selected for cheap reproduction.

ALFRED D. THOMAS: MOSES AND THE DAUGHTERS OF MIDIAN

Exodus 2:15-22

MRS. E. G. MACMILLAN: THE ANNUNCIATION

Luke 1:26-38

Out of the scores of annunciations which artists have given us, many would acclaim Fra Angelico's as having the greatest degree of excellence and insight. He placed his scene in Italy and in a home environment familiar to his eyes; here, the event has a distinctly Indian setting. Note the absence of such symbols as an angel, lily, dove, or ray of light. How much Western symbolism should be mediated to Asiatic and African churches?

ANGELO DA FONSECA: THE ANNUNCIATION

Two murals on either side of the sanctuary door in the chapel of the C.P.S.S. Ashram, Poona, represent the Annunciation—the angel carrying a lotus on the left and the picture reproduced here on the right. The cymbals, the lamp, and Mary dressed as a Maharashtrian girl identify the picture with India. The artist was born in Goa, Portuguese India, studied painting under Dr. A. N. Tagore and Mr. Nandalal Bose, and since 1934 has dedicated himself to religious art.

S. BOSE: THE VISIT OF THE WISE MEN
Matthew 2:1-2

Many Indians believe that one or more of the wise men who visited the Christ Child came from India. Hence, although Persians are here placed in the foreground, beyond them can be seen a priest presenting the trident of Hinduism to the Christ Child. Each is dedicating whatever treasure his life contains to the service of Christ, or to his representative—a little child. The artist is a Hindu by religion, an instructor in the School of Arts and Crafts, Lucknow, and was commissioned by a missionary to paint this picture. It is interesting that it was reproduced in *Madhuri*, a Hindu secular magazine.

ALFRED D. THOMAS: MADONNA AND CHILD

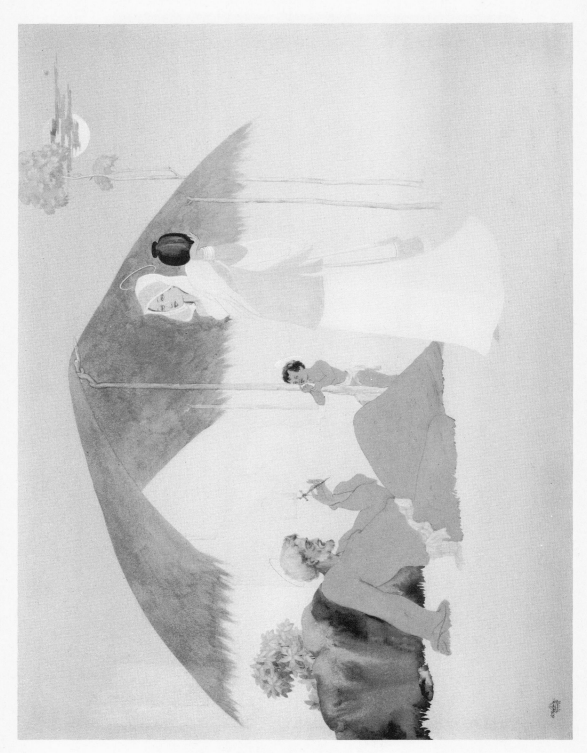

ALFRED D. THOMAS: THE HOLY FAMILY

JOSEPH V. UBALE: THE WOMAN AT THE WELL

John 4:1-30

The artist, recently deceased, was a medalist of the Bombay School of Art.

61

ALFRED D. THOMAS: "COME UNTO ME"

Matthew 11:28

"Come unto me, all ye that labor and are heavy laden, and I will give you rest."

ALFRED D. THOMAS: JESUS STILLING THE WAVES

Mark 4:35-39

ALFRED D. THOMAS: AT THE FOOT OF THE CROSS

Matthew 27:55, 56

This simple and effective picture combines the pathos, the significance and the glory of the Cross. Lines give the mere suggestion of the Himalayas and the round earth. Does this mean that the Cross is for India and, also, for all the world?

64

ALFRED D. THOMAS: CHRIST THE DAWN

This full-size mural representation of Jesus Christ, the Light of the World, dawning upon folk of every caste and creed, was painted (1937) by Mr. A. D. Thomas for Dr. and Mrs. L. H. Beals of Wai, Western India, in memory of their son, and through their courtesy is shown here. At the right, in semi-darkness are Hindu temples. High and low caste, Moslem and Hindu, one blind and one burdened move toward the central Light. Standing in the water is a high-caste widow who begins to understand the meaning of the Light. Leaning upon a crutch is an "untouchable" cripple rapt in adoration of the Light of Love which is even for him. On the left are Christians—men and women of different castes and creeds who have come into His presence. Among them little Theodore Beals offers a flower to a child near by. Our Lord, in glowing white garments, stands upon the rocks above the riverside beckoning lovingly to all men. A tiny yellow flower, springing from the rocks at Jesus' feet, bends in adoration and gives promise of new life and joy and hope.

SION BALA DAS: THIRST

The Master speaks: "You come with your cup to assuage my thirst, but I know your own heart's desire. I accept your devotion and your service—the offerings of your love. Abide in me, and the hunger and thirst of your loving heart will find complete and wondrous satisfaction."

The artist is a gifted teacher in the United Missionary Girls' High School, Calcutta. Her first classes in the school were in the nature of adventures undertaken by teacher and pupils together, for she had not had much training in art. Later on professional art training became available. At the end of the first year she painted this picture based on an incident in *The Hidden Years,* and was awarded a prize for the best picture by a woman in India. Finding that the Hindu influences of the art school stifled her impulse to express her Christian faith in painting, she left the school, and only casual guidance has been available since.

CHRISTIAN ART IN AFRICA

THERE WAS a time when the Negro art of Africa was despised as the expression of an uncultured and inferior race. To all inured to Greek standards of beauty an African statue appeared crude or even disgusting. We looked upon carved gods, masks and weapons merely as curiosities, not as works of art. To the present generation is due, then, the discovery of the highly esthetic aspects of African culture. Within the past forty years European artists of eminent and indisputable authority have acclaimed works by African sculptors and carvers for the masterpieces which they are. Art in Africa appears in metallurgy, plastics, weaving, carving, sculpture and the drama more often than in painting.

This new appraisal is, in part, the result of seeing collections in museums, marvels of patience and skill—spoons finely wrought, staffs of command, canoe paddles elegantly slender, and vessels of all shapes with varied motifs and in hues selected with definite taste. But, in part, the new appreciation has come from the acquired ability on our part to look quite objectively at mask or statue, asking what it is that the carver is trying to say, rather than prejudging it by our techniques and standards. Judged by their own objectives— power to arouse terror in the people—the sculptors of the Congo masks were great masters. Moreover, when one discovers the skill in design shown by African artists, one must conclude that they were not attempting to portray a beautiful human body. Nor, for some reason, were they attempting to reproduce anything exactly; probably no African sculptor ever engaged a model. Evidently they did value clear design, rich pattern, fine surface quality, tremendous solidity and appreciation of volume. Let us not be too quickly provincial in appraising the reproductions which follow.

It is a question whether European recognition of high values in African art may not have come too late. There is danger that her precious inheritance may be lost through lack of appreciation by government and mission.

An even more inhibiting factor for any modern expression of African art is the crumbling of the religious and tribal systems under which the native arts grew up. The power of African art lay in its association with religion. The impact of European and American civilization and the disintegrating effects of scientific attitudes are dispelling the atmosphere of fear and awe. Indigenous belief has become blurred and discredited. Conditions which fostered the

67

older arts are passing away. Of what use would it be to encourage the mere copying of native craftsmanship when the system of thought which inspired it is no more? One must hope that the African's new faith will vitalize his inherited artistic genius, as centuries ago Christianity stimulated art in Europe.

That there is urgent need of a distinctly African Christian art has been eloquently voiced by the Bishop of Masasi in Central Africa. "A copy of Byam Shaw's picture of our Lord appearing in a Zulu hut hangs in the Cathedral of Masasi, and I have seen an African deacon standing in front of that picture with tears on his cheeks, as for the first time he looked at a picture where Africans were near to our Lord." The Bishop reports that Moslems tell Africans that Christianity is a white man's religion and that when Africans see picture after picture representing our Lord, his Mother, the apostles and saints as Europeans, they begin to think the Moslems are right. "For we must remember that the simple African at present regards a picture as a photographic reproduction, made at the time, of what actually took place. It is not always remembered that our European faces are not regarded as beautiful by the African, rather the reverse, and to some are terrifyingly ugly." Manifestly everything within our power should be done to reveal Christianity as belonging equally to the African and to other races.

How can the little that survives of the old cunning of hand be preserved? We can definitely attempt to develop in Africans appreciation of their own art; we can discourage the too docile acceptance of European models; we can stimulate an expectant waiting for a Christian artistic feeling to develop true to Africa as well as to the new faith. In some schools African motifs have been introduced. A few exhibitions have been held. For three years annual prizes amounting to two hundred and fifty dollars have been offered in South Africa for the purpose of encouraging Bantu art and literature.

Some of the pictures which follow show the results of such encouragement. For example, the carving on page 72 is by Job Kekana. The rector of Pietersburg, North Transvaal, went one day to visit this young man in his home kraal and found him carving clever figures with a penknife as his only tool. The work was so promising that Job Kekana was sent for three years to the Diocesan Training College at Pietersburg, where his gifts were developed under the tuition of a sister of the Community of the Resurrection. Canon Stacy Waddy, who longed to see the artistic gifts of every race consecrated to the service of the church, bought the carving represented on page 72 for the

Society for the Propagation of the Gospel in Foreign Parts, London, where it is often used in their little chapel.

The artist who carved the crucifix on page 74 was discovered almost by accident. Nthenge Nthula, a youth of twenty-two, before having attended any school, equipped himself with rude tools with which he could follow an inner urge to carve. For some time he was an itinerant vendor of images of wood. One day he presented himself to the school at Kaboa, in the Vicariate Apostolic of Zanzibar, to sell his works for bread. A priest, noting with what skill he was endowed, invited him to remain.

Manifestly Africa offers a problem for Christian art differing from that of China, Japan or India. But in due time Africa will have a Christian artistic language of her own.

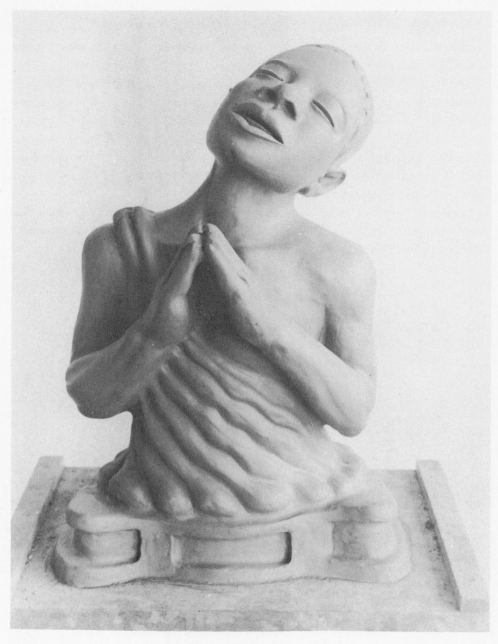

BEN ENWONWU: BOY PRAYING

The creator of this pottery figure was trained as a student by Mr. K. C. Murray of the Nigerian Educational Department, and is now art master in the Government College, Umuahia, Nigeria.

ERNEST MANCOBA: A BANTU MADONNA

The African shows skill in wood carving; but, thus far, relatively little has been done to consecrate this gift to Christian use. An encouraging beginning, however, has been made at the Diocesan Training College, Pietersburg, North Transvaal, where woodwork and carving are taught under the direction of Sister Pauline, C.R. A notable result is this Madonna, four feet high, carved in teakwood by one of the students, as his first large piece of work. Mr. Mancoba is now thirty years of age and is being sent to Europe for two years' further training.

JOB KEKANA: A BANTU CALVARY

John 19:25-27

In this carving, executed by an African Christian (see page 68) from a design by the Reverend E. G. Paterson, it will be noted that all the figures are Bantu in character and dress. Our Lord is an African native with woolly hair. The Virgin Mary is a native girl with a *dook,* or handkerchief, tied round her head such as all the women wear. St. John is wrapped in a blanket only. In the background are African huts on the veldt. This carving is in warm red-toned wood and measures twenty inches high.

A CRUCIFIX-FETISH

This carved wood crucifix, in the possession of the Baptist Missionary Society, London, is two or three hundred years old, and was once used as a fetish in West Africa. Above, one can see the Cross, but the horizontal piece is too high and too short for the arms. These are bound with a stout rope which also fastens the feet. The rope ends upward in a knot upon the neck. The picture does not show how the Savior is fastened to the Cross. The features are peaceful as in sleep and the body seems in repose. Thus, the carver has not portrayed the gripping agony of the worn-out, suspended form which has been caught with realism by European masters. Nevertheless the whole carving breathes reverence for the Savior's person, and is an interesting example of the magic power which the Divine Sufferer had for the native mind. The reverse of the crucifix is shown on the right.

NTHENGE NTHULA: AN AFRICAN CRUCIFIX

Nthenge Nthula (see page 69) naturally carved this crucifix in African style. Whether we of another culture like or dislike this representation is not the significant question. Compare it, for example, with Rubens' "Christ between Two Thieves." Which *to Africans* would convey more meaning? Which would better touch *their* minds and consciences?

A NUN READING HER BREVIARY

Note the simplicity, the elimination of everything which might confuse the effect of symmetry and balance, the full, free, unerring sweep of the circle which bounds the upper part of the body confined in its veil, and the simple oblong of the lower portion with the few vertical corrugations necessary to make the rigid folds of the heavy skirt.

The expression of concentration is secured by squeezing the features into the smallest possible compass in the middle of the broad round face—not by any of the subtle facial modifications that a Western artist would use. The effect is intensified by a small dot for a pupil at each *interior* corner of the narrowed eyes. Manifestly traditions rooted in generations of isolation from the distractions of alien teaching could not be uprooted by the evident presence of a Western model.

ALL CREATURES PRAISING GOD

"All creatures of our God and King
Lift up your voice and with us sing
Alleluia! Umuahia! Alleluia!"

The skill and predilection of the African for carving animals produced this altar carving of iroko, a hard brown wood, in the Government College, Umuahia, Nigeria. Round the edges, not shown in the picture, are the first lines of the college hymn quoted above and adapted from the hymn of St. Francis of Assisi (cf. *Psalms* 148:10-13). The carving is six by three feet. The animal kingdom, ranging from the elephant and crocodile down to spiders, tortoises and beetles, are worshipping their Creator, represented by the central Sun with its rays streaming out to all parts. Only the naughty little bat on the left and the tree bear hanging upside down on the right have not turned their faces toward the sun. The extreme edges of the carving would not, unfortunately, come into the print, so that the man gathering palm nuts from the tree on the left is omitted, as well as the woman standing beneath the tree, and the tortoise behind the elephant. The carver is a native of Benin City, where carving in hard wood has been practised for many years.

76

M. DUPAGNE: ADORING ANGELS

These remarkable sculptures in relief make their immediate appeal and we exclaim, "What beautiful African art!" As a matter of fact they are by a European artist, M. Dupagne, and in 1937 were temporarily decorating the portal of the native chapel of the pavilion of the Congo Belge at the International Exposition, Paris. They may serve, however, to illustrate a problem which presents itself when interested Western artists try to encourage indigenous art in other lands by themselves attempting something in native style. For the artistic traditions of the West cannot easily be laid aside. Try as they may, their works inevitably retain aspects that may be little understood or appreciated by the people.

77

FROM ALL NATIONS

THE PICTURES in this book suggest that cultures and artistries are no longer the separated possessions of isolated peoples. Of deeper significance is the fact that they afford one more evidence that "Christendom" can no longer be identified with the domain of Western Christianity.

The universal and interpenetrating character of our faith is well illustrated by an engraved silver plaque designed by Behzad Minatur, a nationally known painter in Iran and recently converted to Christianity. Part of the symbolism was consciously taken from the Nestorian Stone Tablet, carved in China, A.D. 781. The plaque was presented by the Church of Christ in Iran to the Board of Foreign Missions of the Presbyterian Church in the U. S. A., at its centennial anniversary in 1937. Thus a representation of "the visit of the Wise Men from the East" is designed in Iran, embodies symbolism from China, and is presented to a sister church in America.

It has been difficult to get Christian paintings from the Near East in indigenous style. For centuries Islam has banned pictures, and the Eastern style of illustration has practically died in all Near East countries except Iran where, tiny though the church is, some beginnings are being made by a Christian artist using the Persian miniature style. Persia has always been a little heretical with regard to Islam by being extremely artistic, never dropping through the centuries her art of illumination. There is a real and joyous esthetic feeling when the people of these countries see the beauty of Arabic handwriting.

On the next page is an example of Moslem art applied to a Christian theme. For Islam accepted Jesus as one of the prophets of God; and, in spite of restrictions, Islamic religious art contains much that owes its inspiration to such stories from the Old and New Testaments and from the Apocryphal writings as formed part of the sacred literature of Islam. The Koran describes the birth of Jesus as taking place in a remote and desolate place, not in a stable (Koran 19:22).

THE NATIVITY (*Moslem*)

This sixteenth century picture, unique in conception and execution, represents the Virgin, exhausted and dejected, leaning against a withered date-palm which at her touch bursts into leafage and fruit, and from its roots a stream gushes forth. The new-born baby, wrapped in swaddling clothes, lies on the ground, with a great flame halo of gold, which seems almost to serve as a pillow. (See page 78.)

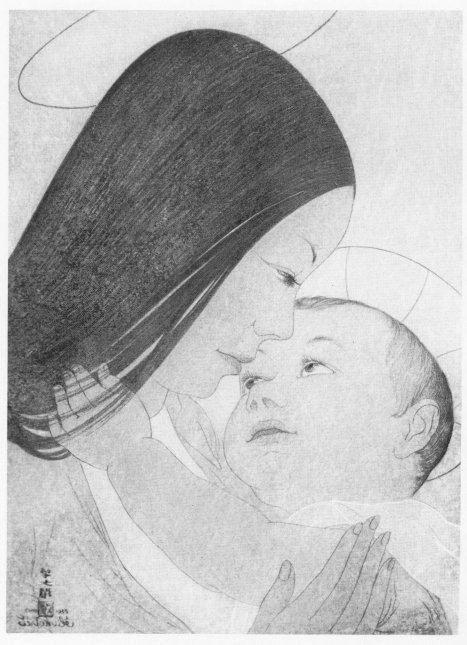

MADONNA AND CHILD (*Indo-China*)

The painter, Lé-van-dé, is a fervent Roman Catholic from Annam (Indo-China) who has studied in Paris, and who has recently done some valuable painting in the Vatican.

THE CHRIST (*Korea*)

The artist, Mr. Ern Ho Kim, is a deacon in the Presbyterian Church, Seoul, and is an active member of the Central (Korean) Y.M.C.A., where this picture is hung. He has studied art both in Seoul and in Tokyo. In this picture, although the figures are Western, Oriental principles of art have been followed in the execution. His pictures have received honorable mention or prizes in exhibitions both in Korea and in Japan.

81

THE LORD'S ACRE (*Siam*)

It is the custom of members of the Petchaburi church, Siam, to set aside the proceeds of a certain ox which is the "Lord's ox," or the eggs from a certain hen which is the "Lord's hen." Boys and girls have dedicated garden plots, also. Offerings are either brought to the church, or the money that results from sales is placed upon the altar. This picture was painted by a young Christian of this church in connection with its campaign for the Lord's Acre Plan. From time to time the Presbyterian mission has attempted to stimulate interest in Christian painting by means of prizes, but the response has come mainly from non-Christian artists.

THE LOST SHEEP (*Mexico*)

Luke 15:3-7

Most of the Christian paintings in Latin America are in the Roman Catholic European style even when by Indian artists. It has been difficult to find anything by Protestants. This picture is one of a dozen on the parables of Jesus by Rolando Zapata, one of the young ministers of Mexico City. His father, one of the older pastors, has always been skillful with his blackboard illustrations, and it is not surprising that his son has produced this series of entirely Mexican pictures which make the parables live before Mexican eyes.

A CHRISTIAN "GOENOENGAN" (*Java*)

The Javanese screen on the opposite page is filled with native Christian symbolism. At the bottom are words which mean, "The discussion of the difficulties and the beauty of art leads up to the consideration of the unity of the Lord and his servant—1934."

The house in the lower foreground is man's inward life, the abiding place of the Lord. Of the two monstrous creatures which guard the door, one carries a sword and the other a jug containing the water of life. Woe unto him who does not respect the sanctuary of the Lord; he will be killed by the sword.

The peacock on the roof, by a play on Javanese words, indicates that man must live near to God. The eagle (Christ's power) and the serpent (Satan) are seen fighting. The eyes of the eagle express consciousness of victory, whereas the shape of the serpent's eyes shows he realizes the coming defeat.

The apes and ravens toward the top are servants of Satan and announce death. The serpent has taken hold of the tree, which in Javanese is designated by the same word as for "will." Thus the human will is in the power of Satan and is unable to follow the will of God until Jesus Christ (the eagle) comes to destroy the serpent and to restore the relation between man and God—a battle which has to be taken over by Christ's followers. Even though man is in the power of Satan, yet the cross at the top means that there is a Savior.

The macrocosmos is symbolized by the four elements—earth (in red at the bottom); water (in blue in the form of waves on either side of the roof); fire (on both sides of the waves); and wind (in the form of leaves and flowers at the top of the lower half of the picture).

The artist is Mr. Atmowidjono, an expert in Javanese mysticism, and a native of Solo, the main center of Javanese culture. He is a qualified puppet player, also. *Goenoengans* are used to separate the different scenes in a play.

Date Due

MAY 1 2 '58	MAR 7 5		
OCT 1 3 '58			
AUG 3 1 '59			
AUG 3 1 '59			
AUG 3 1 '59			
RESERVE *Missions*			
Due 11/12			
FEB 1 7 '66			
SEP 1 6 '66			
RESERVE			
Christianity in India			
MAR 22 '68			
APR 5 '68			
MAY 3 '68			
10/110/94	23233